explore Investing.(Innovate, Strategize, and Maximize Returns)

NARTAN TYAGI

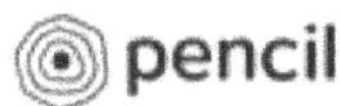

ISBN 978-93-5667-856-9

Published in India 2023 by Pencil

A brand of
One Point Six Technologies Pvt. Ltd.
Unit no. 26, Ground Floor, Building A1,
Wadala Truck Terminal Road,
Near Post Office, Antop Hill, Mumbai - 400037
E connect@thepencilapp.com
W www.thepencilapp.com

DISCLAIMER: *The opinions expressed in this book are those of the authors and do not purport to reflect the views of the Publisher.*

Author biography

NARTAN TYAI a seasoned financial expert and renowned author, has dedicated [his/her] career to empowering individuals with the knowledge and tools to achieve financial success. With a passion for educating and guiding others, [Your Name] has become a trusted resource in the field of personal finance and investment.

he has a unique ability to distill complex financial concepts into accessible and actionable insights, making [his/her] writing relatable and relevant to readers from all walks of life. he has a talent for breaking down intricate investment strategies, risk management techniques, and psychological aspects of finance, allowing readers to make informed decisions and navigate the dynamic world of finance with confidence.

CONTENTS

Chapter 1 The Evolution of Investing From Traditional to Modern Approaches

Introduction: In the world of investing, strategies and techniques have continually evolved over time. This chapter delves into the historical development of investing, tracing the journey from traditional approaches to the advent of modern investment strategies. By understanding this evolution, investors can gain insights into the changing landscape of investment opportunities and make informed decisions in today's dynamic markets.

1.1 The Traditional Investment Landscape:

Exploration of traditional investment vehicles, such as stocks, bonds, and mutual funds.
Overview of the conventional buy-and-hold approach and the dominance of fundamental analysis.
Historical perspective on traditional investing and its limitations in capturing new opportunities.

1.2 Technological Disruption and the Rise of Modern Investing:

Introduction to the transformative impact of technology on the investment landscape.
Examination of the democratization of investing through

explore Investing.(Innovate, Strategize, and Maximize Returns)

online trading platforms and discount brokerages.
Rise of algorithmic trading and its influence on market efficiency and volatility.

1.3 The Emergence of Quantitative and Systematic Strategies:

Overview of quantitative investing and the use of mathematical models and algorithms to drive investment decisions.
Discussion of systematic strategies, including trend following, factor investing, and smart beta.
Evaluation of the benefits and challenges associated with these data-driven approaches.

1.4 Innovations in Risk Management and Portfolio Optimization:

Introduction to modern risk management techniques, such as value at risk (VaR) and stress testing.
Exploration of portfolio optimization methodologies, including mean-variance optimization and risk parity.
Discussion of how these advancements have enhanced investors' ability to construct diversified and risk-controlled portfolios.

explore Investing.(Innovate, Strategize, and Maximize Returns)

1.5 The Rise of Passive Investing:

Examination of the growth and popularity of passive investing, particularly through index funds and exchange-traded funds (ETFs).
Analysis of the debate between active and passive investing and their respective merits.
Consideration of the impact of passive investing on market efficiency and pricing dynamics.

1.6 The Integration of Environmental, Social, and Governance (ESG) Factors:

Introduction to the integration of ESG factors into investment decision-making.
Discussion of how ESG considerations have gained prominence as investors increasingly focus on sustainability and responsible investing.
Exploration of the various approaches and frameworks for incorporating ESG factors into investment strategies.

1.7 Looking Ahead: The Future of Investing:

Insight into emerging trends and technologies shaping the future of investing.
Consideration of the impact of artificial intelligence, machine learning, and big data on investment practices.
Examination of regulatory challenges and ethical considerations in an evolving investment landscape.

explore Investing.(Innovate, Strategize, and Maximize Returns)

Conclusion:This chapter has provided a historical overview of investing, tracing its evolution from traditional approaches to the modern investment landscape. By understanding the advancements, disruptions, and emerging trends, investors can adapt their strategies to capitalize on new opportunities and navigate the complexities of the ever-changing investment world. Recognizing the significance of this evolution is crucial for staying informed and making well-informed investment decisions in today's dynamic markets.

Chapter 2 Introduction to Investing

Introduction:Investing is a fundamental tool for wealth creation and financial growth. This chapter serves as an introduction to the world of investing, providing essential knowledge and insights to set the foundation for successful investment strategies. It covers the basics of investing, including key concepts, investment vehicles, and the importance of aligning financial goals with risk tolerance.

1.1 The Power of Investing:

Investing possesses a transformative power that goes beyond simple saving or relying solely on earned income. It offers the potential for exponential growth and the opportunity to generate wealth over time. By allocating funds into investment vehicles, individuals can leverage their capital to earn returns and create a pathway to financial prosperity. Here are further elaborations on the power of investing:

1.1.1 Building Wealth: Investing allows individuals to accumulate wealth by putting their money to work. Unlike traditional savings accounts that often offer minimal interest rates, investing in assets such as stocks, bonds, or real estate presents the possibility of higher returns. Over the long term, these returns can contribute significantly to wealth creation, providing a means to fund major life goals, such as buying a home, retiring comfortably, or securing financial freedom.

1.1.2 Beating Inflation: Investing is a tool to combat the erosive effects of inflation. Inflation erodes the purchasing power of money over time, meaning that the same amount of money will buy fewer goods and services in the future. By investing in assets that tend to outpace inflation, such as stocks or real estate, investors have the potential to preserve and grow their wealth, ensuring that it maintains its value over the long run.

1.1.3 Generating Passive Income: Investing can generate passive income streams that provide financial stability and independence. Rental properties, dividend-paying stocks, or interest-bearing bonds are examples of investments that can yield regular income. This passive income can supplement earned income and provide financial security, especially during retirement or periods of reduced work activity.

1.1.4 Capital Appreciation: Certain investments, such as stocks or real estate, have the potential for capital appreciation, where the value of the asset increases over time. By investing in assets that appreciate in value, individuals can experience capital gains, which can significantly enhance their overall investment returns. Capital appreciation can result from factors such as market demand, technological advancements, or business growth.

1.1.5 Financial Freedom and Opportunities: Investing opens up doors to financial freedom and opportunities that may not be possible through traditional means. It can provide the resources to start a business, pursue higher education, or take advantage of new ventures. By accumulating wealth through investing, individuals gain the ability to make choices based on their interests and aspirations, rather than being solely driven by financial constraints.

1.2 Understanding Investment Vehicles:

To embark on a successful investing journey, it is crucial to have a solid understanding of different investment vehicles and their characteristics. Various investment options exist, each with its own risk and return profile, liquidity, and investment horizon. Here, we delve deeper into the concept of investment vehicles:

1.2.1 Stocks: Stocks, or equities, represent ownership in a company. Investing in stocks involves purchasing shares of publicly traded companies, which can be listed on stock exchanges. Stocks offer the potential for high returns, but they also come with higher risk compared to other investment options. Investors can analyze a company's financials, industry trends, and market conditions to make informed decisions about buying, holding, or selling stocks.

1.2.2 Bonds: Bonds are debt instruments issued by governments, municipalities, or corporations to raise capital. When an investor buys a bond, they are essentially lending money to the issuer in exchange for periodic interest payments and the return of the principal amount at maturity. Bonds are generally considered lower risk compared to stocks, as they provide fixed income and have defined maturity dates. The risk associated with bonds primarily lies in the issuer's creditworthiness and potential changes in interest rates.

1.2.3 Mutual Funds: Mutual funds pool money from multiple investors to invest in a diversified portfolio of stocks, bonds, or other assets. They are managed by professional fund managers who make investment decisions on behalf of the investors. Mutual funds offer diversification, as they typically hold a variety of securities, reducing the impact of any single investment's performance on the overall fund. Investors can choose from different types of mutual funds based on their investment goals, risk tolerance, and time horizon.

1.2.4 Exchange-Traded Funds (ETFs): ETFs are similar to mutual funds in that they hold a diversified portfolio of assets. However, unlike mutual funds, ETFs trade on stock exchanges like individual stocks. ETFs provide flexibility, as they can be bought and sold throughout the trading day at market prices. They offer diversification, transparency, and typically have lower expense ratios compared to mutual funds. ETFs cover various asset classes, including stocks, bonds, commodities, and more.

1.2.5 Real Estate: Investing in real estate involves purchasing properties, such as residential homes, commercial buildings, or land, with the goal of generating income and/or capital appreciation. Real estate investments can provide both ongoing rental income and potential long-term appreciation. They offer diversification benefits and can act as a hedge against inflation. Real estate investment options also include real estate investment trusts (REITs), which allow investors to participate in real estate ownership without directly owning properties.

1.2.6 Other Investment Vehicles: Beyond the aforementioned investment options, there are various alternative vehicles available to investors. These include hedge funds, private equity, venture capital, commodities, precious metals, and cryptocurrencies. Alternative investments often have higher risk and require a deeper understanding of their unique characteristics and market dynamics. They can provide opportunities for higher returns but may come with limited liquidity and higher entry barriers.

1.3 Setting Financial Goals:

Before embarking on an investing journey, it is vital to establish clear financial goals that provide direction and purpose for your investments. Setting meaningful and achievable goals helps shape your investment strategy, risk tolerance, and time horizon. Here, we delve deeper into the importance of setting financial goals:

1.3.1 Clarity and Focus: Setting financial goals brings clarity to your investment objectives. It allows you to define what you want to achieve with your investments and provides a focus for your investment decisions. Whether your goals include buying a house, funding education, retiring comfortably, or achieving financial independence, having clearly defined goals helps you stay motivated and make decisions aligned with your long-term vision.

1.3.2 Measurability and Accountability: Financial goals should be measurable to track progress and hold yourself accountable. By quantifying your goals, such as saving a specific amount of money, achieving a target return on investment, or accumulating a certain net worth, you can evaluate your progress over time. This measurability provides a sense of accomplishment as you reach milestones and reinforces the discipline required for successful investing.

1.3.3 Realistic and Achievable: Setting realistic financial goals is crucial to avoid setting unrealistic expectations or taking on excessive risk. Goals should be attainable based on your financial situation, income, expenses, and investment resources. It is essential to consider factors such as time horizon, expected returns, and market conditions when setting goals. A balance between ambition and feasibility ensures that your goals remain within reach and increases the likelihood of achieving them.

1.3.4 Short-Term and Long-Term Goals: Financial goals can be categorized into short-term and long-term objectives. Short-term goals typically span one to three years and may include building an emergency fund, saving for a vacation, or paying off debt. Long-term goals extend beyond three years and often involve retirement planning, funding higher education, or creating a sustainable income stream. Distinguishing between short-term and long-term goals helps prioritize your investment decisions and allocate resources accordingly.

1.3.5 Flexibility and Adaptability: Financial goals should be flexible to accommodate changes in your personal circumstances or external factors. Life events, such as marriage, career changes, or unexpected expenses, may require adjustments to your goals. It is important to regularly review and reassess your goals to ensure they remain relevant and attainable. Flexibility allows you to adapt your investment strategy as needed without compromising the overall vision.

1.3.6 Aligning Risk Tolerance: Financial goals and risk tolerance go hand in hand. Understanding your risk tolerance, which is the level of uncertainty and potential loss you are comfortable with, is essential in setting goals that align with your risk profile. Conservative goals may prioritize capital preservation and steady income, while more aggressive goals may involve higher-risk investments with the potential for greater returns. Aligning your goals with your risk tolerance helps strike a balance between potential rewards and the level of risk you are willing to bear.

1.4 Risk and Reward:

Risk is an inherent part of investing, and understanding the risk and reward tradeoff is crucial for making informed investment decisions. By assessing risk, considering risk tolerance, and employing risk mitigation strategies, investors can manage and navigate the uncertainties of the market effectively. A well-balanced approach that aligns risk with financial goals and time horizons is key to achieving optimal investment outcomes. It is important to strike a balance between risk and reward, considering both the potential for growth and the potential for losses, to build a resilient and successful investment portfolio.

explore Investing.(Innovate, Strategize, and Maximize Returns)

1.5 Investment Time Horizon:

Explanation of the concept of investment time horizon and its impact on investment strategies.
Discussion on short-term investments, medium-term investments, and long-term investments.
Guidance on aligning investment choices with the appropriate time horizon based on financial goals.

1.6 Market Basics:

Introduction to key market concepts, such as supply and demand, market cycles, and volatility.
Explanation of how market conditions affect investment performance.
Overview of the factors influencing market trends, including economic indicators, geopolitical events, and investor sentiment.

1.7 Investment Strategies:

Introduction to different investment strategies, including buy-and-hold, value investing, growth investing, and income investing.
Overview of the importance of diversification and asset allocation in managing risk and maximizing returns.
Guidance on selecting investment strategies that align with individual financial goals and risk tolerance.

1.8 The Importance of Research and Education:

Emphasis on the significance of research and continuous education in successful investing.

Introduction to reliable sources of financial information, including financial news, books, online resources, and professional advice.

Discussion on the benefits of staying informed about market trends, investment opportunities, and evolving investment strategies.

Conclusion:This chapter has provided an introductory overview of investing, emphasizing its power in building wealth and achieving financial goals. By understanding the basics of investment vehicles, risk-reward dynamics, financial goal setting, and market fundamentals, readers are equipped with a solid foundation for making informed investment decisions. Remember, investing is a journey that requires continuous learning and adaptation to changing market conditions, and this chapter sets the stage for the subsequent exploration of various investment strategies and vehicles.

chapter 3 Stocks and Equities

2.1 Introduction: Stocks, also known as equities, are one of the most well-known and widely traded investment vehicles. Investing in stocks allows individuals to become partial owners (shareholders) of publicly traded companies, providing the opportunity to participate in their growth and share in their profits. This chapter explores the fundamentals of stocks and equities as an investment option.

2.2 Ownership and Dividends: When investors purchase stocks, they acquire ownership stakes in the underlying companies. As shareholders, they have certain rights, including the right to vote on major company decisions and the potential to receive dividends. Dividends are a portion of a company's profits distributed to shareholders as cash payments or additional shares. Dividends can provide a regular income stream for investors, especially those seeking stable income.

2.3 Types of Stocks: There are various types of stocks available in the market, each with its own characteristics and considerations. Common stocks are the most prevalent type and provide ownership and voting rights to shareholders. Preferred stocks offer priority in receiving dividends and potential liquidation proceeds but generally do not carry voting rights. Growth stocks belong to companies with high growth potential but may not pay dividends initially. Value stocks are typically undervalued by the market and have the potential for price appreciation.

2.4 Stock Exchanges and Markets: Stocks are traded on organized exchanges, such as the New York Stock Exchange (NYSE) or NASDAQ, where buyers and sellers come together to transact. These exchanges provide a regulated and transparent marketplace for investors. Additionally, there are over-the-counter (OTC) markets where stocks trade directly between parties. The stock market is influenced by various factors, including economic conditions, industry trends, geopolitical events, and company-specific news.

2.5 Risks and Volatility: Investing in stocks comes with inherent risks and volatility. Stock prices can fluctuate due to various factors, including market conditions, company performance, regulatory changes, and investor sentiment. The value of stocks may decrease, resulting in potential capital losses. It is important for investors to assess their risk tolerance, diversify their portfolios, and adopt a long-term perspective when investing in stocks.

2.6 Fundamental Analysis and Valuation: Investors often use fundamental analysis to evaluate stocks and determine their intrinsic value. Fundamental analysis involves examining a company's financials, including revenue, earnings, debt levels, and growth prospects. Valuation methods, such as price-to-earnings (P/E) ratio, price-to-book (P/B) ratio, and discounted cash flow (DCF) analysis, help investors assess whether a stock is overvalued, undervalued, or fairly priced.

2.7 Technical Analysis and Market Timing: Technical analysis focuses on analyzing historical price and volume patterns to make investment decisions. Chart patterns, trend lines, and technical indicators are used to identify potential buy or sell signals. Market timing, based on technical analysis, aims to predict short-term price movements and take advantage of short-term trading opportunities. It is important to note that technical analysis has its limitations and should be used in conjunction with other investment approaches.

2.8 Long-Term Investing and Patience: Stock investing is often associated with a long-term investment horizon. Stocks have historically delivered solid returns over extended periods, but short-term fluctuations are common. Long-term investors benefit from compounding growth and the ability to ride out market volatility. Patience and discipline are key attributes for successful long-term stock investing.

Chapter 4 Bonds and Fixed Income Investments

3.1 Introduction: Bonds and fixed income investments play a crucial role in investment portfolios, offering investors the opportunity to generate stable income and preserve capital. This chapter explores the fundamentals of bonds and fixed income investments, providing insights into their characteristics, types, and benefits.

3.2 Bond Basics: Bonds are debt instruments issued by governments, municipalities, or corporations to raise capital. When investors purchase bonds, they are essentially lending money to the issuer in exchange for periodic interest payments and the return of the principal amount at maturity. Bonds have predefined terms, including the coupon rate (interest rate), maturity date, and face value. They are generally considered lower risk compared to stocks, as they provide fixed income and have defined cash flows.

3.3 Types of Bonds: There are various types of bonds available to investors, each with its own features and considerations. Government bonds, such as U.S. Treasury bonds, are issued by governments to finance public projects and are considered low-risk investments. Municipal bonds are issued by state and local governments to fund infrastructure projects and offer tax advantages for investors. Corporate bonds are issued by corporations and vary in risk depending on the creditworthiness of the issuer. Other types of bonds include convertible bonds, which can be converted into company stock, and high-yield bonds, also known as junk bonds, which offer higher yields but come with higher risk.

3.4 Coupon Payments and Yield: Bonds generate income through periodic coupon payments, which represent the interest paid to bondholders. The coupon rate is specified at the time of issuance and is usually fixed for the life of the bond. Bond yields, such as current yield and yield to maturity, reflect the total return an investor can expect from a bond, considering both coupon payments and potential capital gains or losses upon maturity.

3.5 Bond Ratings and Credit Risk: Credit rating agencies assign ratings to bonds based on the issuer's creditworthiness and the likelihood of timely repayment. Common rating agencies include Standard & Poor's (S&P), Moody's, and Fitch Ratings. Higher-rated bonds, such as those with AAA or AA ratings, are considered lower risk and typically offer lower yields. Lower-rated bonds, such as those with BB or below ratings, carry higher credit risk and offer higher yields to compensate investors for the increased risk.

3.6 Bond Pricing and Market Factors: Bond prices are influenced by various factors, including interest rates, inflation expectations, and market conditions. When interest rates rise, bond prices generally decline, as newly issued bonds offer higher coupon rates. Conversely, when interest rates fall, bond prices tend to rise. Understanding the relationship between bond prices and market factors is essential for investors to make informed decisions regarding buying, holding, or selling bonds.

3.7 Bond Ladders and Strategies: Bond laddering is a strategy that involves diversifying bond holdings across different maturities. By spreading investments across various bonds with different maturity dates, investors can manage interest rate risk and maintain a regular income stream. Other bond strategies include barbells, bullet strategies, and immunization strategies, which cater to specific investment goals, risk tolerance, and market conditions.

3.8 Bond Funds and Exchange-Traded Funds (ETFs): Investors can gain exposure to bonds through mutual funds or exchange-traded funds (ETFs). Bond funds pool investors' money to invest in a diversified portfolio of bonds, offering convenience and professional management. ETFs, on the other hand, trade on stock exchanges like individual stocks and provide flexibility and transparency. Bond funds and ETFs offer access to a wide range of bonds, making them suitable for investors seeking broad fixed income exposure.

Chapter 5 Real Estate Investments

4.1 Introduction: Real estate investments have long been considered a tangible and potentially lucrative asset class. Investing in real estate involves acquiring properties or investing in real estate-related securities to generate income and achieve capital appreciation. This chapter explores the fundamentals of real estate investments, including types of properties, investment strategies, and benefits.

4.2 Types of Real Estate Investments: Real estate investments encompass various property types, each with its own characteristics and investment potential. Residential properties, such as single-family homes, apartments, and condominiums, offer the opportunity for rental income and potential long-term appreciation. Commercial properties, including office buildings, retail spaces, and industrial warehouses, can provide income through leases with businesses. Other real estate investments include vacant land, vacation rentals, real estate investment trusts (REITs), and real estate development projects.

4.3 Rental Income and Cash Flow: Investing in income-generating properties allows investors to earn rental income. Rental properties provide a steady cash flow stream, as tenants pay monthly rent. Cash flow can be enhanced by careful property selection, rental market analysis, and effective property management. Positive cash flow occurs when rental income exceeds expenses, while negative cash flow implies expenses exceed rental income. Analyzing cash flow is crucial for evaluating the profitability of real estate investments.

4.4 Appreciation and Equity Growth: Real estate investments have the potential for capital appreciation over time. As demand for properties increases or market conditions improve, property values may rise, allowing investors to realize a profit upon sale. Appreciation can be influenced by factors such as location, economic growth, infrastructure development, and supply and demand dynamics. Additionally, as mortgage debt is paid down, equity in the property increases, building wealth for the investor.

4.5 Leverage and Financing: Real estate investments offer the opportunity to leverage capital through financing. Borrowing money, such as obtaining a mortgage, allows investors to acquire properties with a smaller upfront investment. Leverage can amplify returns when property values increase, but it also carries risks if market conditions decline. Understanding the risks and rewards of leveraging capital is crucial in real estate investing.

4.6 Real Estate Market Analysis: Analyzing the real estate market is essential for making informed investment decisions. Factors such as supply and demand dynamics, local market conditions, rental rates, vacancy rates, and economic indicators should be considered. Conducting market research and due diligence helps identify potentially profitable investment opportunities and minimizes the risk of investing in areas with unfavorable market conditions.

4.7 Property Management and Maintenance: Effective property management is vital for successful real estate investments, particularly for rental properties. Proper tenant screening, rent collection, property maintenance, and addressing tenant concerns are key responsibilities of property managers. Investors can choose to self-manage their properties or hire professional property management companies to handle day-to-day operations.

4.8 Real Estate Investment Strategies: Real estate investment strategies vary based on individual goals, risk tolerance, and market conditions. Strategies include buy-and-hold, where investors acquire properties for long-term appreciation and rental income. Fix-and-flip involves purchasing distressed properties, renovating them, and selling them quickly for a profit. Real estate investment trusts (REITs) offer the opportunity to invest in a diversified portfolio of properties through publicly traded securities. Other strategies include real estate crowdfunding, property development, and vacation rentals.

4.9 Tax Benefits and Considerations: Real estate investments offer several tax advantages that can enhance returns. Deductible expenses, such as mortgage interest, property taxes, and maintenance costs, can reduce taxable income. Additionally, depreciation allows investors to deduct a portion of the property's value over time. It is important to consult with tax professionals to understand the specific tax implications and benefits of real estate investments.

Chapter 6 Mutual Funds and Exchange-Traded Funds (ETFs)

5.1 Introduction: Mutual funds and exchange-traded funds (ETFs) have gained immense popularity as investment vehicles that offer diversification, professional management, and accessibility to a wide range of investors. This chapter delves into the fundamentals of mutual funds and ETFs, exploring their structure, benefits, and considerations for investors.

5.2 Understanding Mutual Funds: Mutual funds pool money from multiple investors to invest in a diversified portfolio of securities, such as stocks, bonds, or a combination of both. They are managed by professional fund managers who make investment decisions based on the fund's objectives. Mutual funds offer various types, including equity funds, bond funds, balanced funds, and sector-specific funds. Investors buy shares or units of the mutual fund, and the fund's value is determined by the net asset value (NAV) of its underlying holdings.

5.3 Benefits of Mutual Funds: Mutual funds offer several advantages to investors. First, they provide instant diversification by holding a basket of securities, reducing the impact of individual stock or bond performance on the overall investment. Second, they are professionally managed, allowing investors to benefit from the expertise and research capabilities of fund managers. Additionally, mutual funds offer liquidity, as investors can typically buy or sell shares on any business day at the NAV price. They also provide accessibility to a wide range of asset classes and investment strategies.

5.4 Considerations for Mutual Fund Investors: When investing in mutual funds, investors should consider factors such as the fund's investment objective, risk profile, past performance, expense ratio, and fund manager's track record. It is important to align the fund's objective with personal investment goals and risk tolerance. Evaluating fees and expenses associated with the fund, such as management fees and sales charges, is crucial to understand the impact on investment returns. Reviewing historical performance and fund manager tenure helps assess the fund's consistency and potential for future success.

5.5 Introduction to Exchange-Traded Funds (ETFs):ETFs are investment funds traded on stock exchanges, similar to individual stocks. They offer investors exposure to a diversified portfolio of securities, mirroring an underlying index or asset class. ETFs can track various benchmarks, such as stock market indices, bond indices, commodities, or specific sectors. Like mutual funds, ETFs provide diversification and professional management, but they offer additional advantages, including intraday trading flexibility, lower expense ratios, and tax efficiency.

5.6 Benefits of ETFs:ETFs offer several benefits to investors. Their ability to be bought and sold throughout the trading day at market prices allows for greater flexibility and liquidity. ETFs generally have lower expense ratios compared to mutual funds, making them cost-effective investment options. Furthermore, ETFs provide transparency, as their holdings are disclosed on a daily basis, enabling investors to see the underlying securities. ETFs also offer the opportunity to implement various investment strategies, including short selling and options trading.

5.7 ETF Structures and Types: ETFs can be structured as either physical or synthetic. Physical ETFs hold the actual securities that comprise the index they track, while synthetic ETFs use derivatives and swap agreements to replicate the index's performance. ETFs come in different types, including equity ETFs, bond ETFs, commodity ETFs, sector ETFs, and international ETFs, allowing investors to gain exposure to specific market segments or asset classes.

5.8 Considerations for ETF Investors: Investors considering ETFs should evaluate factors such as the ETF's tracking error, liquidity, bid-ask spreads, and underlying index methodology. Tracking error measures the deviation between an ETF's performance and the index it aims to replicate. Higher liquidity and narrower bid-ask spreads enhance trading efficiency. Understanding the underlying index's construction

Chapter 7 Retirement and Tax-Advantaged Investing

Introduction: Preparing for retirement is a crucial financial goal for individuals seeking financial security and independence in their golden years. In Chapter 7, we delve into the realm of retirement and tax-advantaged investing, exploring various strategies and vehicles that can help individuals maximize their savings while minimizing their tax liabilities. From individual retirement accounts (IRAs) and 401(k) plans to annuities and Social Security, this chapter provides valuable insights into the importance of planning for retirement and taking advantage of tax-efficient investment options.

Section 1: The Importance of Retirement Planning
1.1 Understanding Retirement Planning

The significance of retirement planning for long-term financial security
Common challenges and obstacles faced during retirement
The impact of inflation and longevity risk on retirement savings

explore Investing.(Innovate, Strategize, and Maximize Returns)

1.2 The Benefits of Early Retirement Planning

The power of compounding and the advantage of starting early

Maximizing retirement savings through disciplined savings habits

The psychological and emotional benefits of a well-planned retirement

Section 2: Tax-Advantaged Retirement Accounts
2.1 Individual Retirement Accounts (IRAs)

Traditional IRAs: Contributions, tax deductibility, and distribution rules

Roth IRAs: Tax-free growth and tax-free qualified distributions

SEP IRAs and SIMPLE IRAs: Retirement options for self-employed individuals

2.2 Employer-Sponsored Retirement Plans

401(k) plans: Features, contribution limits, and employer matching

403(b) plans: Retirement options for employees of nonprofit organizations

Thrift Savings Plan (TSP): Retirement plan for federal employees

explore Investing.(Innovate, Strategize, and Maximize Returns)

2.3 Health Savings Accounts (HSAs)

Combining healthcare and retirement savings with HSAs
Triple tax advantages and qualified medical expense requirements
Strategies for maximizing HSA contributions and investment growth

Section 3: Annuities and Lifetime Income
3.1 Annuities as Retirement Vehicles

Understanding the basics of annuities and their types
Fixed annuities: Guaranteed income streams and protection against market volatility
Variable annuities: Market exposure and potential for higher returns

3.2 Social Security and Pension Plans

Navigating the complexities of Social Security benefits
Maximizing Social Security by understanding claiming strategies
Pension plans: Defined benefit vs. defined contribution plans

explore Investing.(Innovate, Strategize, and Maximize Returns)

Section 4: Tax-Efficient Investing Strategies
4.1 Asset Location and Allocation

Optimizing tax efficiency through strategic asset placement
Identifying tax-efficient investments for taxable and tax-advantaged accounts
Balancing risk and return while considering tax implications

4.2 Tax Loss Harvesting and Capital Gains Management

Utilizing tax loss harvesting to offset capital gains
Managing capital gains through strategic selling and asset allocation
Understanding wash-sale rules and other tax considerations

Section 5: Estate Planning and Inheritance
5.1 Estate Planning Essentials

The importance of estate planning in preserving wealth
Utilizing trusts, wills, and power of attorney documents
Estate tax considerations and strategies for minimizing tax liabilities

explore Investing.(Innovate, Strategize, and Maximize Returns)

5.2 Inheritance and Beneficiary Designations

Understanding the impact of beneficiary designations on estate distribution
Strategies for minimizing taxes on inherited retirement accounts
Estate planning considerations for blended families and charitable giving

Chapter 8 International and Global Investing

Introduction: In an increasingly interconnected world, investing beyond domestic borders has become essential for investors seeking to diversify their portfolios and capitalize on global opportunities. Chapter 8 delves into the realm of international and global investing, exploring the benefits, challenges, and strategies associated with investing in foreign markets. From understanding foreign exchange markets and assessing country-specific risks to navigating international mutual funds and exchange-traded funds (ETFs), this chapter provides valuable insights into the exciting world of international investing.

Section 1: The Case for International Investing
1.1 Understanding International Investing

Differentiating between international and domestic investing
Benefits of international diversification for risk management
Opportunities for higher returns and exposure to emerging markets

explore Investing.(Innovate, Strategize, and Maximize Returns)

1.2 The Impact of Globalization on Investment Opportunities

Globalization's influence on trade, commerce, and investment
Growth of multinational corporations and global supply chains
The interconnectedness of economies and its implications for investors

Section 2: Evaluating International Markets and Risks
2.1 Assessing Country-Specific Risks

Political and regulatory risks in foreign markets
Economic stability and currency risk considerations
Understanding cultural differences and their impact on investments

2.2 Analyzing Global Economic Trends

Identifying macroeconomic factors affecting international markets
Analyzing GDP growth, inflation, and interest rate differentials
Geopolitical events and their potential impact on global investments

explore Investing.(Innovate, Strategize, and Maximize Returns)

2.3 Currency Risk Management

Understanding the role of foreign exchange markets
Evaluating currency risk and its impact on investment returns
Hedging strategies and currency overlay techniques

Section 3: Investment Vehicles for International Exposure
3.1 International Mutual Funds and ETFs

Exploring the benefits and drawbacks of international funds
Passive vs. active management approaches in global investing
Evaluating fund performance, expenses, and diversification

3.2 Global Depositary Receipts (GDRs) and American Depositary Receipts (ADRs)

Investing in foreign companies through depository receipts
Advantages and risks of GDRs and ADRs
Considerations for selecting individual depository receipts

3.3 Emerging Markets and Frontier Markets

Understanding the opportunities and risks in emerging markets

explore Investing.(Innovate, Strategize, and Maximize Returns)

Evaluating investment options in frontier markets
Country selection and diversification strategies in developing economies

Section 4: Practical Strategies for International Investing
4.1 Sector and Theme Investing

Capitalizing on sector-specific opportunities across countries
Identifying global investment themes and megatrends
Evaluating sector-focused ETFs and mutual funds

4.2 Portfolio Allocation and Rebalancing

Determining optimal allocation to international investments
Rebalancing strategies to maintain desired exposure
The role of home bias and overcoming it in portfolio construction

4.3 Due Diligence and Research Considerations

Conducting in-depth research on international markets
Evaluating country-specific factors and economic indicators
Leveraging expert opinions and resources for informed decision-making

Chapter 9 Risk Management and Portfolio Allocation

Introduction: Effective risk management and strategic portfolio allocation are fundamental components of successful investing. Chapter 9 explores the crucial concepts of risk management and portfolio allocation, providing readers with the tools and knowledge necessary to build resilient portfolios that balance risk and reward. From understanding different types of risk and their implications to implementing diversification strategies and asset allocation techniques, this chapter equips investors with the essential skills to navigate the complex world of investment risk.

Section 1: Understanding Investment Risk

1.1 Types of Investment Risk

Market risk: Systematic and unsystematic risk factors

Credit risk: Assessing the creditworthiness of investments

Interest rate risk: Impact of changes in interest rates on investments

Liquidity risk: The ability to buy or sell an investment without impacting its price

Currency risk: Exchange rate fluctuations and their effects on investments

1.2 Risk-Return Tradeoff

Exploring the relationship between risk and potential returns

Assessing risk tolerance and establishing investment objectives

The role of time horizon and financial goals in risk management

Section 2: Diversification and Asset Allocation
2.1 Importance of Diversification

Understanding the benefits of diversification in risk reduction

Correlation analysis and the impact on portfolio diversification

The role of different asset classes in diversifying risk

2.2 Asset Allocation Strategies

Strategic asset allocation: Establishing long-term target allocations

Tactical asset allocation: Adjusting allocations based on market conditions

Alternative asset allocation: Including non-traditional assets in the portfolio mix

explore Investing.(Innovate, Strategize, and Maximize Returns)

2.3 Modern Portfolio Theory (MPT)

The principles and assumptions of MPT
The efficient frontier and optimal portfolio construction
Capital Asset Pricing Model (CAPM) and its role in asset allocation

Section 3: Risk Management Techniques
3.1 Risk Identification and Measurement

Identifying and assessing portfolio risks
Volatility, standard deviation, and other risk metrics
Stress testing and scenario analysis for risk evaluation

3.2 Risk Mitigation Strategies

Hedging strategies: Using derivatives to offset specific risks
Stop-loss orders and risk control mechanisms
Insurance products and their role in risk management

3.3 Portfolio Rebalancing and Monitoring

The importance of regular portfolio rebalancing
Triggers for rebalancing based on asset class performance
Monitoring and adjusting portfolios to maintain risk targets

Section 4: Behavioral Aspects of Risk Management
4.1 Investor Behavior and Decision-Making Biases

Understanding common behavioral biases in investing
Overcoming emotional biases and making rational decisions
The role of discipline and patience in risk management

4.2 The Role of Professional Advisors

Benefits of working with financial advisors and wealth managers
Selecting the right advisor and establishing a trusting relationship
Regular communication and collaboration with advisors for risk management

Chapter 10 Investor Psychology and Emotional Discipline

Introduction: Investing is not just about numbers and financial analysis; it also involves understanding the complex realm of human psychology and emotions. Chapter 10 delves into the fascinating field of investor psychology and emotional discipline, shedding light on the psychological biases and behavioral patterns that can influence investment decisions. By exploring strategies to manage emotions, cultivate discipline, and make rational choices, this chapter aims to empower investors to overcome common pitfalls and achieve long-term success in their investment journeys.

Section 1: The Role of Psychology in Investing
1.1 Understanding Investor Psychology

Cognitive biases and their impact on investment decisions
Emotional influences on decision-making processes
The role of investor sentiment and market psychology

1.2 Behavioral Finance and its Implications

Exploring the intersection of finance and psychology
The limitations of traditional finance theories
Insights from behavioral finance research

explore Investing.(Innovate, Strategize, and Maximize Returns)

Section 2: Common Biases and Emotional Traps
2.1 Confirmation Bias

Seeking information that confirms pre-existing beliefs
Overlooking contradictory evidence and potential risks
Strategies to mitigate confirmation bias

2.2 Loss Aversion

The tendency to feel the pain of losses more than the pleasure of gains
Impact on risk tolerance and portfolio decisions
Techniques to manage loss aversion and maintain a long-term perspective

2.3 Herding Behavior

The tendency to follow the crowd and conform to group decisions
The influence of social media and news on herding behavior
Maintaining independence and avoiding herd mentality

Section 3: Emotional Discipline and Decision-Making Strategies
3.1 Cultivating Emotional Discipline

Recognizing and managing emotions in investment decisions

explore Investing.(Innovate, Strategize, and Maximize Returns)

Practicing patience and avoiding impulsive actions
Techniques for staying focused during market volatility

3.2 Goal Setting and Investment Planning

Establishing clear financial goals and investment objectives
Creating a well-defined investment plan to guide decision-making
Aligning investments with personal values and long-term aspirations

3.3 Risk Management and Asset Allocation

Implementing risk management strategies to limit emotional biases
Constructing a diversified portfolio based on individual risk tolerance
Regularly reviewing and rebalancing portfolios to maintain desired allocations

Section 4: Seeking Professional Guidance and Support
4.1 The Role of Financial Advisors

Benefits of working with a trusted financial advisor
Leveraging expertise and objective guidance
Collaborating with advisors to manage emotions and make informed decisions

explore Investing.(Innovate, Strategize, and Maximize Returns)

4.2 Developing a Support System

Engaging with a community of like-minded investors
Sharing experiences and insights with peers
Seeking support during challenging market conditions